George's War Then and Now

A Great-Granddaughter Reflects

Beth Lindsay Templeton

Greenville, S.C.

Also by Beth Lindsay Templeton

Loving Our Neighbor:
A Thoughtful Approach to Helping People in Poverty

Understanding Poverty in the Classroom:
Changing Perceptions for Student Success

Angelika's Journal:
What You Can Do about Poverty and Homelessness

A Coat Named Mr. Spot

Conversations on the Porch:
Ancient Voices – Contemporary Wisdom

More Conversations on the Porch:
Ancient Voices – Contemporary Wisdom

Refrigerator Prayers for Ordinary People

The Christmas Strawberry…and Other Stories

Uncharted Journey:
On the Challenges of Getting Older and Other Transitions

The Sacred Year

**George's War
Then and Now**

Copyright © 2021 Beth Lindsay Templeton

All rights reserved. No part of this book may be used or reproduced by any means, graphic, electronic, or mechanical, including photocopying, recording, taping or by any information storage retrieval without the written permission of the publisher except in the case of brief quotations embodied in critical articles and reviews.

Published by:

FpS

1175 Woods Crossing Rd., #2
Greenville, S.C. 29607
864-675-0540
www.fiction-addiction.com

ISBN: 978-1-945338-89-2

Cover & Book Design by Vally Sharpe
Author Photograph by the author's late husband, Jim Banks

Printed in the United States of America.

George F. Robertson

The Bookshelf

A Small Boy's Recollections of the Civil War—George F. Robertson. Standard Printing Company.

As each year diminishes the number of people who were actual witnesses to the Civil War, descriptions of those stirring days are most interesting. George F. Robertson, who was a member of the class of 1878 at Davidson College, has written his recollections of the Civil War and presents them in entertaining fashion.

Mr. Robertson was born in 1853 on a farm near Greeneville, Tennessee, and as a boy witnessed much Civil War activity. His father was a newspaper editor and published in several towns in the South. From the viewpoint of an alert boy he saw the events which he narrates in an informal and good-natured manner. The story is told from memory of actual happenings. He tells how the Confederate proclamation for volunteers brought men to the stars and bars, the first flag of the Confederate States. He points out that the first soldier to fall in battle during the Civil War was a soldier from North Carolina. Long train loads of soldiers passed through Greeneville on the way to the Virginia battlefields, sleeping on beds made from straw thrown on the floors of the box cars.

In every town there were Northern sympathizers and some of these were bold enough to do violence to the Southern force by burning bridges and by other deeds.

The small boys of the time had exciting experiences. They would walk out to the camps so they could water the horses of cavalry companies. Both sides were guilty of foraging, an unavoidable result of the war. The author narrates an incident where some soldiers took cooking vessels from the kitchen of his mother and how he, a young boy, received permission from the Commandant to go about the tents in search of his family's property. Sometimes old muskets were left behind by the soldiers and these fascinated the boys as guns always interest the young boy.

Once while his family was living in Wytheville, Virginia, the townspeople were horrified to see a blue streak moving along the road that led into the town. Fearing a Northern raid, the town was in bedlam. But the troops proved to be Confederate soldiers who had raided the Yankee commissary stores, and needing the captured coats, proceeded to wear them.

Robertson was with a small wagon train that crossed over the mountains from Wytheville to Asheville. The men loaded their wagons with salt which they offered to the mountain folk or "bush-wackers." It was in autumn and the young boy ate apples and chinquapins to his heart's content.

"I saw three great movings of humanity during the war and immediately at its close. Burnside's army on the march, Longstreet's grand army review and the negro hegira immediately after their realization of the fact they were free. I'll never forget that sight."

At Asheville the author went to a private school of Colonel Stephen Lee, and some years later to Captain Banks at Newton Academy where he was prepared for Davidson College.

Contents

Preface xi

THEN 1
War! War! 3
Trains In and Out of Greeneville 6
War Challenges and Troubles 9
Matters in General 11
In Yankee Lines 13
Yankees Out, Rebels In 17
In Yankee Lines Again 20
On to Wytheville 23
Chinkapins and Apples 27
War to the Finish 30

NOW 35
A Great-Granddaughter Reflects 37

Acknowledgments 43
About George F. Robertson, D.D. 45
About Beth Lindsay Templeton 47

Preface

In 1932, my great-grandfather, George F. Robertson, wrote and published a book reflecting his memories from his childhood during the Civil War. Titled *A Small Boy's Recollections of the Civil War,* it sat on the shelves of family members, including mine, for several years. It was mostly there for me as a monument to his literary accomplishments.

What began as a simple writing project to take my great-grandfather's book and bring it back using current language and idioms became an unexpected quest. I learned that the Civil War was more than battles. George never witnessed any gun fights even though he saw troops of both sides moving in and out of his hometowns.

Then, when I realized my great-great-grandparents had owned three house and yard servants who were enslaved, I was shaken. About the time that piece of information began to deeply resonate in my white heart, racial tensions exploded in the United States. My great-grandfather's little tale of his memories as an eight-year-old boy during the Civil War became a jumping off point for a soul-searching process that continues to this day.

Before I go on, though, you should read my adaptation of his words for yourself.

"In a real sense all life is interrelated. All men are caught in an inescapable network of mutuality, tied in a single garment of destiny. Whatever affects one directly affects all indirectly. I can never be what I ought to be until you are what you ought to be, and you can never be what you ought to be until I am what I ought to be. This is the inter-related structure of reality."

— Rev. Martin Luther King, Jr. —

George's War
Then and Now

THEN

1
War! War!

I—George Robertson—was eight years old on April 23, 1861. Just a few months before, our neighbor, South Carolina, had become the first slave state to secede from the United States of America.

Everyone in my hometown of Greeneville, Tennessee waited to learn what was going to happen next. What were the northern leaders holding Fort Sumter in the Charleston Harbor going to do? Would they respond to General Beauregard's third and final demand to surrender the fort? Would Tennessee vote to secede?

We children did not play our usual games that day. Men

> **The state of South Carolina voted to leave the United States on December 20, 1860. Between January and December 1861, 11 more would states would secede. On February 4, the states formed a separate government from the U.S., known as the Confederacy.**

gathered in small groups to discuss the potential terrors that might happen. The tension broke a bit when eight young men rode through the town waving the Palmetto flag of South Carolina. No one knew if the fellows were for or against the Confederacy.

George's War, Then and Now

Finally, the suspense was over. We learned the fort had been fired on. War was declared soon after that.

The men of east Tennessee did not hurry to sign up as soldiers to fight under the Confederate flag, the Stars and Bars. Many in our part of the country were against secession. Some people slipped into Kentucky to become Union soldiers. Others who left lived there until after the war.

My father was the editor of the *Greeneville Democrat* newspaper. The paper supported Andrew Johnson's political ambitions. However, after Tennessee seceded on June 8, 1961 and joined the Confederacy, Father joined the Southern army.

People all around him were not happy with this action. Father decided that becoming a Confederate soldier was a better way to protect his family. Later people appreciated his actions. The state legislature gave Father a walking cane on whose gold head were written these words:

"To H.G. Robertson, an Honest Champion of Civil Rights, from Members of the Legislature and Other Citizens of Tennessee."

But back to the story. My dad, now *Captain* Robertson, continued to print his newspaper, now named *The Southern Banner*. He also served as Post Quartermaster in Greeneville. This job made him responsible for providing quarters, rations, clothing, and other supplies.

Confederate troops were stationed in Greeneville. My buddies and I loved watching the troops drill. We boys created our own company, too. We used pieces of board cut into the shape of a gun. We created our own flag, named officers, and drilled and

A Great-Granddaughter Reflects

drilled. Every one of us vowed we would have joined the army if we had been old enough.

My brother, Will, even though he was only seventeen, slipped away to become an actual soldier. Will was sent to Vicksburg, Mississippi, to protect the Mississippi river from Yankee gunboats moving up or down stream.

One regiment stationed in Greeneville was from North Carolina. While they drilled, a fifer and drummer played the only song he knew...over and over. The townspeople quickly tired of hearing the sad, sad song. I thought it sounded like a dying cow.

A measles epidemic broke out in the camps south of town. The government took over the East Tennessee Eating House, the Vance House, the Wright Hotel, the Female Academy, and Andrew Johnson's house to use as hospitals.

I saw the death wagons roll by our house carrying the bodies of soldiers who died from measles. Greeneville College, on the north side of town became a smallpox hospital.

I watched the standard bearers with their drooping flags lead the funeral procession for an officer. Next came a band playing a funeral march. A caisson carrying the body followed. Then came soldiers in full uniform. Two files of soldiers on each side of the grave fired their guns into the air and then the funeral was over.

2
Trains In and Out of Greeneville

Trains came through town carrying soldiers to the battlefields in Virginia. The only beds were straw spread on the floors of the box cars. Each soldier had a blanket but no pillow or sheet.

My friends and I loved to watch the trains pass. We enjoyed even more finding knives on the ground that fell from the train while the soldiers slept.

My friends and I sold items to the soldiers on the trains. Fruits and chestnuts, when they were in season, were always good sellers. We sold cakes and pies. I sold cigars.

Trains also came to Greeneville from the battlefields, filled with wounded soldiers. The women in the town brought tubs of water and bandages to care for the men. Doctors met the trains to sew up wounds and send the men on their way. They took those who were too wounded to travel to the hospitals.

Other trains brought Yankee prisoners. The Yankees were allowed to get off in Greeneville. The captives used their two-hour stop to walk around the town. They visited with Union sympathizers in town. People gave them food and other things to help them.

A Great-Granddaughter Reflects

> Confederate soldiers were called "Rebels." Because the Confederate soldiers' uniforms were gray, they were often called "boys (or men) in gray."
>
> Soldiers in the U.S. Army, also known as the Union Army, were called "Yankees." Union soldiers were also known as "blue bellies" because the jackets of their uniforms were blue.

One Union prisoner came into our yard and asked Mother for something to eat. My eyes were huge because this was the first Yankee I had ever seen.

My younger brother, Bob, asked the man, "Are you a Yankee?"

The man smiled and said, "I guess I am. That's what they call me."

Bob looked the man up and down and then asked, "Have you got a blue belly?"

Bob and I had heard older men refer to the Union soldiers as "blue bellies." I did not hear the prisoner's answer but I, too was curious about those blue stomachs!

Trains also came through Greeneville carrying cannons—one cannon to each long flat car. When one train stopped, I climbed up for a better look at the monster gun. Its wide mouth encouraged me to inspect the cannon even more closely. I slipped down into the cannon, feet first. I lay there a moment thinking about how strange the situation was. Then the train began moving.

I began moving, too! Had I been a bigger boy or the cannon smaller in size, I might have been scared even more than I was. But I got out in time!

One day, Father took me to see a special train that was passing through Greeneville. It was carrying one of the Confederate's generals, General Price.

When the general stepped down from the train, Father introduced me. I felt like I was standing in greatness when

George's War, Then and Now

General Price patted me on my head. No other boy in Greeneville had such an honor.

General Sterling Price

3
War Challenges and Troubles

Certain items were hard to get because of the war. People especially missed good coffee. Some of the Union women promised everyone would once again have good coffee when the Yankees came. Mother and the other ladies made "coffee" from dried apples cut into small pieces and parched, from rye grain grown on the farms, or from sweet potatoes. They even made coffee from North Carolina chestnuts.

When the Yankees took over Greeneville for a time, the ladies did indeed get some imported coffee. The Yankees made their coffee from whole beans and then sold the ladies the dried leftovers. The women used these remains to make a cup of coffee. It was not as good as they had hoped. However, it was better than what they had been drinking.

The women missed having nice clothes. Unless they had a bolt of cloth stored from before the war, they had no fine dress material. They made over old dresses. They added trim in every way possible to make the dresses feel "new." The women used logwood, copperas, madder, homegrown indigo, barks and roots to make dyes to change their dresses. They were able to get cotton cloth from the cotton mills for white goods and domestic items. The ladies knew how to card and spin the wool from local sheep to make jeans and flannels. One of my aunts even made for herself a silk dress from real silk from cocoons.

At that time a calico dress had fourteen yards of fabric. One lady proudly announced to Mother that she had just finished sewing a dress with only ten yards of calico. Think of it!

One group in town called Tories were Union sympathizers. They did not enlist in the Union army. Some of them prowled around the town searching for items of value they could steal. Tories went to my aunt's house and ripped up her feather beds. They took her daughters' elegant and expensive cashmere shawls with rich embroidery. They spread these beautiful things over their horses, between the animal and the saddle. I heard stories of things they did to people when searching for hidden money.

During the war, people on the Union side of the conflict burned bridges. They did not want the Confederate army to move their soldiers and supplies easily. The Confederates declared bridge burning a crime punishable by death. Two men were captured and proclaimed that they would burn more bridges if they ever got away. They were sentenced to death.

On the day of their punishment, the two men were walked up Depot Street surrounded by a square of Confederate soldiers. People, including me, lined both sides of the streets. The prisoners crossed the railroad tracks just west of the depot and walked to the edge of the woods. Two ropes were hanging from a tree there. After everything was all over, I wished with all my heart that I had not been there to see what I saw. It was horrid and caused nightmares for many nights. Nevertheless, there were no more bridge burnings in east Tennessee.

4
Matters in General

My friends and I liked the military cavalry best because it had horses. Since there were no water faucets in the camp, someone had to take the horses to a stream about a mile away from camp. We boys were more than eager to help out. We'd often walk the first half mile with the horses. We'd ride the second half mile as we headed to the stream.

I made friends with a soldier whose horse, Billy Button, was too small to really be called a horse and too large to be a pony. Because of our friendship, I was allowed the privilege of taking Billy Button to the stream whenever I could slip away from Mother's watchful eye. One Sunday, the guys and I decided that we would have a horse race.

I barely knew how to ride a horse much less race one. However, Billy Button knew exactly what to do. He flew like an arrow in the air. He flattened himself out and outran every living creature. I hung on, hoping and hoping that I would not die. Billy Button and I won. I decided that was my first and last horse race.

We boys had political differences just as our parents did. Some were Rebels and others were Yankees. We fought as boys, never as Rebel and Yankee soldiers. However, the Yankee boys did have one sure way to beat their Rebel friends. They quoted Bible verses that promised victories to the North and none to the South. We Rebel boys did not know if they used the verses accurately or not, but we could not defend ourselves. We just had to grin and bear it. We all continued to attend the same churches that we did before the war.

One night it snowed about four or five inches in Greeneville. Some of the soldiers who were from south Georgia had never seen snow. They yelled and screamed and shouted and made all kinds of racket. They wrestled, rolled and tumbled, fought battles with snowballs, washed faces, and crammed snow down each other's back. They were boisterous and loud but enjoyed that battle of fun in the midst of a war.

5
In Yankee Lines

Without any fighting at all, Greeneville moved from being held by Rebels to coming under Yankee control. It was not until the Yankees had permanent possession of east Tennessee that there was any fighting at or near Greeneville. I could hear cannons in the fight at Bulls Gap and also at Big Creek near Rogersville, Tennessee, but none near my town. Just before the Yankees came, Father left with the army.

The Yankees took control of Father's printing press which was on the ground floor of our home. They printed their leaflets and other papers there. Mother and my little brother Bob were not happy at all to have Yankee soldiers in our house. Bob would try to "attack" the soldiers. They would holler at him and he'd run back upstairs. From that safe place, he would pretend to fight the entire Yankee army!

The soldiers took good care of the press but when they finally left, they took an important part with them. The press was unable to be used. Later when our press foreman returned, he whittled a wood replica of the missing piece which was then made into the metal part. The press was up and running again with few problems.

George's War, Then and Now

One day a Yankee officer came to Mother and ordered her to prepare dinner for ten officers. My mother did not like at all being ordered about in that way. It really stung her. But she made a good, honest dinner which they enjoyed. However, during the meal, the officers talked about how the Rebels were cowards and how they would whip them good. They bragged about being able to eat Christmas dinner in their own homes up north that very same year.

Mother thought in her heart that her dinner guests did not realize they were fighting patriots...not Rebels. These patriots were fighting for the Constitution of the United States of America which guaranteed to every state in the Union the right to withdraw from the Union. Even so, Mother held her head high in the midst of the officers' abusive talk.

Afterwards the leader came to Mother and said, "We are very much obliged to you, madam, and suppose you are obliged to us." She never figured out what she was supposed to be obliged to them for. At least they took only the meal and no household items.

One morning when Mother was milking a cow, a Yankee soldier walked up to take some of the feed meant for the cow. She recognized the soldier as Sam, one of the Greeneville young men who'd ridden through the town the day Fort Sumter was captured. She said, "Sam, you are not going to take my feed, are you?"

"Don't the feed belong to the Confederacy, Mrs. Robertson?"

"No, it is my own."

"I'll not take it, then." He left.

Another Yankee soldier came a few days later. The same thing happened. He asked, "Where is your husband, madam?"

"He's with the army."

A Great-Granddaughter Reflects

"Oh...then I'll take it all." And he would have, too, except that he was unable to carry all the feed.

A number of Rebel prisoners were held in the old freight depot on the hill just above our house. They were southern sympathizers, not soldiers. Mother could see the comings and goings from her living room window. One of her friends, Mrs. Davis, wanted to see her husband who was locked up. However, the officer in charge refused her permission to enter.

Mrs. Davis happened to see the Yankee General Burnside leaving the prison, so she ran up to him. He stopped and heard her complaint. The General turned around and shouted loud enough for all to hear: "Let this lady see her husband whenever she wishes." Mother still did not care for Yankees, but she greatly approved of General Burnside. His action showed he had a heart.

General Ambrose Burnside

One Sunday I was sitting on the porch of the hotel on Main Street dangling my bare feet over the edge of the sidewalk when General Burnside's unit began marching through town. Even though I did not like Yankees, I loved seeing the drilling and marching. These soldiers were equipped with new uniforms. They had fresh guns, new flags, and regimental banners. I was so enchanted that I forgot to go home for Sunday dinner. Even though I missed eating, I was glad that I did not have to sit and listen to Mother's Sunday teaching.

Just as the Yankees had come without a fight, they left the same way. I climbed on the roof of my front porch to watch the

George's War, Then and Now

procession as columns of soldiers marched out of town. I was so excited all I could say was, "The Yankees is retreatin', the Yankees is retreatin'." Mother tried to get me to hush but I was too excited. I later marveled that no one had shot me off the roof!

With the Yankees gone, Father could return home.

6
Yankees Out, Rebels In

We Robertsons once again saw the Stars and Bars and gray uniforms in town.

One day I heard a commotion. Soldiers were marching through the streets in full uniform and equipment. Their uniforms and flags showed wear and tear.

General James Longstreet

The troops marched four men across north through Main Street. When they passed the college, they turned up a narrow alley which led to a long, narrow field surrounded by woods. Soldiers filled the field almost as far as my buddies and I could see. They were preparing for a grand army review by General Longstreet. When the General passed each company, they presented arms. When he passed a band, and there were several, the musicians gave a musical salute. When this happened, the general's horse reared and pranced. I laughed out loud. After the general and his staff had

George's War, Then and Now

gone the entire length of the line of soldiers, the troops were ordered back to camp.

When the Yankees had left Greeneville, they left several muskets that my friends and I picked up. We also found ammunition. We had no use for the guns but, of course, the guys and I had to try them out.

Every musket had an iron ramrod with screw threads on one end. Gun wipers attached to the end. To use the wiper, cotton or other soft fabric had to be wrapped around the end after it was attached to the ramrod.

I loaded my musket but discovered to my horror that the wiper had detached from the ramrod about halfway up the barrel. I now had a loaded gun with something fastened in the barrel that might make the gun burst. I was afraid to fire the gun because I could not get the wipers out.

One of the guys offered to fire the gun if I would give him some powder. I made the trade. The boy took the gun to the fence. All of us stood well back because we feared tragedy. The shooter raised the gun to his shoulder, but accidentally pulled the trigger too soon. The gun roared like a cannon and kicked like an army mule. My friend doubled over in pain but when he could speak he said what the we already knew: the gun did not burst into pieces and he was still alive!

The Rebel soldiers soon relieved us of our guns. The troops surely needed them more than we children did! I know that every mother breathed a sigh of relief.

The Rebels disappeared mysteriously again from Greeneville. One day Mother heard a man call hello at the back door. She went to the door and found a Confederate general and his staff on their horses in the back yard. The general introduced himself as General Vance.

A Great-Granddaughter Reflects

"Madam, do you know where any Yankees are?"

"No, sir, I do not, but I would advise you to get away from here as soon as possible."

"Why do you advise that, madam?"

"I do not know, sir, but my advice is for you to get out of town as quickly as possible."

He thanked her and left.

It was very good that General Vance paid attention to Mother's intuition. He went out Buncombe Road toward Asheville, North Carolina, and was hardly out of town before the Yankees came in by every other road.

General Vance unfortunately was captured in Jefferson County not too long after leaving Greeneville. A Yankee officer saved the general from being stabbed to death by a bayonet held by an old German Tory.

Gen. Robert B. Vance after the war
Photo taken between 1865 and 1880
by celebrated photographer Mathew Brady

7
In Yankee Lines Again

The Yankees came back to town with no special demonstration, battle, or even gun fire. This occupation of Greeneville by the Yankees was the last one of the war. There was never fighting in or very near Greeneville.

There was once a small skirmish downtown when a Rebel soldier fell off his horse just as Yankees were pushing the Rebels back. The Rebel ran into the basement of the Wright Hotel. A lady living in the Tory-owned hotel happened to see the Rebel slip in. She sent some local children to the basement to find the soldier. They did not discover him.

The lady said, "I'll find him" and went into the room. The soldier was hiding behind a column. When the lady moved, he moved. She was disappointed in her search. When the Rebels moved back in front of the hotel, the soldier darted out, jumped on another horse with a soldier, and escaped.

One day a Yankee came to Mother and demanded some flour from her. Fortunately, he did not want all that she had. She picked up an empty flour sack to put the soldier's flour into. Because it was full of holes, the soldier tried his best to close the leaks.

A Great-Granddaughter Reflects

"Haven't you a better sack than this?"

"I have none for you." (In her mind, Mother emphasized the words "for you.")

He took the bag she offered. Mother indeed had other bags but not for him.

Of all the things of the war experience, what bothered Mother most was how soldiers just appeared at her home asking or demanding food or other things. One day an officer with his sword and a squad of eight men in full uniform came right into her kitchen.

The second lieutenant grandly entered this "Rebel holdout" that was occupied with just Mother and three boys. The lieutenant announced with great formality that they wanted some cooking vessels. The soldiers bore these trophies of war away in triumph!

I was ten. I went alone to see the Yankee Commandant and told him what had happened. The Commandant listened very kindly and gave me a written order to take whatever I could identify.

I went through the camp asking to see the cooking vessels. The soldiers were very young and obviously new recruits. Yet they treated me kindly and showed me the vessels. I saw so many that looked just like the ones taken from our house that I left empty-handed.

One Saturday afternoon, one of the leading ladies of Greeneville was baking cookies for her children. A passing Yankee was reminded of "home and mother" as he passed the house with its sweet scent. He went to the kitchen and asked the lady for some cookies. She promptly and positively refused to give him any. She said, "You Yankees have taken nearly everything we have. Out of what is left, I am making these cookies for my children. I'll give you none."

George's War, Then and Now

The soldier threatened to take the cookies anyway. The lady lifted her rolling pin, saying, "If you don't get out of here in a hurry, I'll knock your #%&* head off." He left.

Later the baker told Mother that she'd gotten so mad that the curse word just slipped out of her mouth before she knew it. But she saved the cookies for her children.

One day six or eight men came into the printing office and took a large marble imposing stone. This particular piece of equipment was essential for making up printing forms. It took six men to carry it away. They also took a large dry press which flattened newspaper sheets until they were dry. They took everything to a neighboring town. My brother Will saw the press in use in its new home.

The Yankees used a two-room building on the corner of my family's lot. The soldiers prepared food in our backyard. I was fascinated with how the cook made flapjacks. He would stir a large pan of batter. Then he poured some into a large, thin, iron frying pan and placed it on the fire. When the underside of the cake was done, the man ran a knife all around the edge of the half-cooked cake. Then the cook gave the pan a twist, tossing the cake into the air, where it cut a flip, after which it would fall batter-side down, kerflop into the pan. When the batter was all used up, the pile of flapjacks seemed to me to be a foot high. Then the soldiers began an assault on the tower of flapjacks. They used butter, gravy, or molasses, wiping their mouths with the backs of their hands.

8
On to Wytheville

Our family decided that if the Yankees returned to Greeneville, we would move east for safety. We left on the last train east to leave Greeneville. We stopped in Bristol, Tennessee for several days in late March 1864.

While there, I saw General Longstreet's soldiers covered with snow trudging along the railroad tracks in retreat.

Father had been ordered to set up his office in Wytheville, Virginia. He put us on the train to Wytheville on April 1.

Father rented a house in the northwestern part of Wytheville. The Yankees had already visited the town, leaving many burned buildings behind them. They swore that if they ever returned to Wytheville, they would burn the rest of the town to the ground.

Our house looked over the Tazewell Road which led southwest from Wytheville. We could see for a mile down the road. One day a blue streak appeared in the road and moved toward town. Women screamed, children cried, and dogs barked. Confusion was everywhere. People feared the Yankees were returning to fulfill their promise to burn down the town.

Then the people noticed that the blue streak did not move with intensity. No, they were riding rather leisurely. The blue

George's War, Then and Now

streak turned out to be a company of Rebel cavalry. They had raided a Yankee wagon train loaded with overcoats. These fellows needed the coats and proceeded to wear them.

A meadow with a creek was across from my school. We built dams there. One day two boys approached me and my brothers. The younger of the boys was about my age while the other one was twelve or thirteen. These two had a reputation of being fighters. But being from another school, I anticipated no trouble.

However, one morning when I was driving our cow to pasture, I met the boys. One of them picked a fight and soon we were at each other with both fists. The boy's big brother stepped in. Then my friend joined the fight. I boasted later, "I gave him all he was looking for and then some. He soon was willing to quit, and I guess I was satisfied with my fighting qualities."

I became known as the "champeen" of Wytheville. I had won my own war!

The town of Wytheville was divided by an east-west line near the water pump. Boys on either side created their own armies. "Captors" took whatever was in the "prisoner's" pockets. For prisons, we used brick ash houses, about four by six feet with a small square door in one end. These little houses were on almost every lot in town and easily guarded by one boy. For guns we used the butts of muskets cut to about twelve inches. We loaded these with powder and lead and shot them in our battles.

The war between us boys got so bad and dangerous, the town authorities stepped in and declared peace. We were glad because even though we had tired of the game, neither side wanted to call a truce or surrender. So, we all laid down our arms.

Yankees came to Crockett's Cove about seven miles from Wytheville. They were firmly entrenched. The town's residents heard some gunfire with Rebel soldiers, but there were few

A Great-Granddaughter Reflects

casualties. Then Rebel General John H. Morgan arrived. His reputation preceded him. When the Yankees learned that General Morgan was about to attack, the Yankees turned and ran away, disobeying orders to stand and fight.

During the last night of his life, General Morgan slept in the house of Mrs. Carrie Williams, who had a magnificent vineyard. The General was not well guarded. In fact, when his trusted scout, Lieutenant Wilbur Carter, sent a dispatch to General Morgan's chief of staff saying, "The enemy is advancing on the Warrensburg Road," the chief refused to believe the message, saying, "No force on earth could march on such a night as this." He threw the message on the floor and went to bed.

A young boy, Leidy, rode a horse he was trying to save from the Rebels to the Yankees at Bull Gap. He told them where General Morgan was.

When the Yankees surrounded the Williams' home, General Morgan ran out of the house. He hid under a grape arbor. When he was called to surrender, he shouted, "I will die first." He did not want to return to a Yankee prison.

General John Hunt Morgan

(June 1, 1825 - September 4, 1864) Born in Kentucky, Morgan did not originally support the secession of Kentucky. When his brother Tom began to support the Confederacy, John also joined. He was killed in Greeneville, Tennessee.

He fired but before he could fire again, a bullet struck him and ended his life. The Yankees threw his body across a horse and then dumped him into a mudhole.

George's War, Then and Now

General Morgan's body was rescued and brought to Mrs. Williams' home and prepared for burial. The body was given to Captain J.J. McAfee and his escort to return to Mrs. Morgan in Abingdon, Virginia.

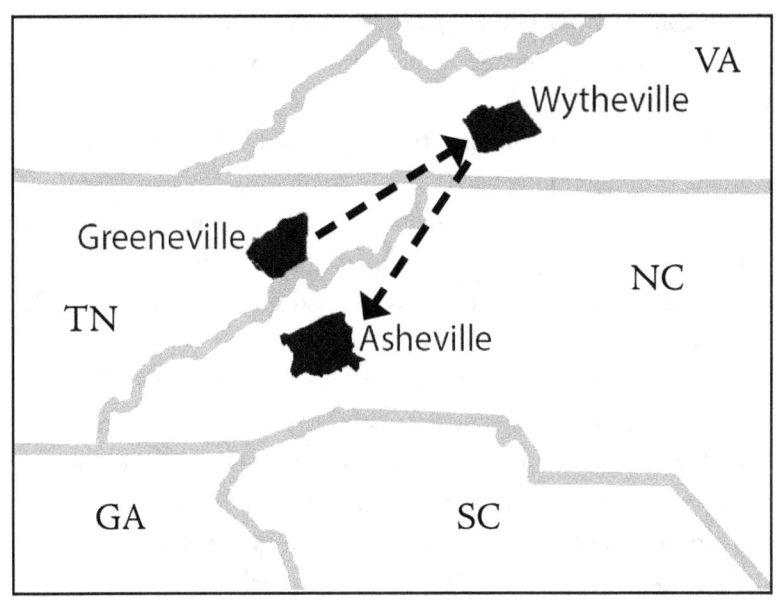

9
Chinkapins and Apples

Father received orders to move to Asheville, North Carolina, so he moved our family with him. Mother and my youngest brother, Bob, rode the train to Asheville. Marcus and I went with the two four-horse wagons that carried the household goods and one two-horse wagon that was loaded with salt. The salt was used as payment for bushwhackers along the route.

The September trip was beautiful through the mountains. The apple crops were abundant and there were millions of chinkapins, a kind of chestnut. One of the horses got sick and could not pull the wagon. Another horse replaced him in the team. We boys were allowed to ride the recuperating horse as it walked alongside the wagon.

Four men, all soldiers, two boys, twelve horses, and three wagons traveled along roads where apples trees were abundant. The apples were all sizes, sorts, and colors. There were Buffs, Blacks, Limbertwigs, Winter Johns, Steins, and others. I could easily have eaten a peck a day. I also enjoyed eating all the chinkapins that I could gather.

After the cavalcade passed through Independence, Virginia, we were in bushwhacker country. Bushwhackers ambushed travelers and took whatever they wanted. One of the soldiers spied men with guns running across the road. The group stopped, my brother and I hid behind the wagon, and the soldiers readied their guns. But we never saw any bushwhackers.

When our caravan came to a cabin on the mountain side, an elderly man came out and asked what we were loaded with. "Salt." The soldiers gave him some salt and went on. They also sold salt along the way to help people out.

George Livingston, one of the waggoneers, lived along the route. He had a comfortable cabin. The war had not hurt him and his family very much. Mr. Livingston was a very clever, good man, and Baptist preacher. His wife offered my brother and me a new kind of coffee from the seed of the sorghum sugar cane. I thought it the best I'd had in long time.

When we finally arrived in Asheville, Mother, Father, and Bob were there to meet us. We lived in a long brick house about one hundred yards from where Merrimon Avenue turns off North Main Street. Father set up his office on Biltmore Avenue. Marcus and I began attending a private school in Chunn's Cove taught by Stephen D. Lee, a distant relative of General Lee.

A Great-Granddaughter Reflects

We Robertsons enjoyed life in Asheville with its large Methodist college for young women, Captain S.M. Banks's Preparatory School, and Colonel Lee's private school. The courthouse was outstanding for a community of one thousand people. The town was a "genuine Southern" town with culture and refinement. Camp Patton, a Rebel garrison, was under the command of General Martin.

10
War to the Finish

The Rebel forces quietly left Asheville. Father, too, left to go behind Yankee lines.

Toward the end of the war, both sides declared a sixty-day armistice. After the Rebels had been gone for a while, a large force of Yankee cavalry passed through the town as quietly as if they were not on hostile soil. My friends and I, along with various ladies of the community, got great views from our front porch. The soldiers passed by about forty feet in front of us, marching two abreast.

The parade took all day. Several times officers would stop at the porch, sometimes to ask for a drink of water, but more likely to engage with the curious women. The men were gentlemen in every way and were well-behaved.

In just a few days after the parade, the armistice was over. Mother frantically called me home from our next-door neighbor's. The sixty-day armistice had expired. The same Yankees who had passed through the town so quietly just a few days before were now coming as an armed, hostile force. They appeared at every door at the same time, pounding for admission. When inside, they rushed around, their sabers rattling against the

A Great-Granddaughter Reflects

floor with noisy clanging, heavy boots stamping like horses... creating bedlam.

When the Yankees entered our home, the only thing they took was some of Mother's fine dried beef.

It was not unusual to ask military authorities to send a guard to watch a home for the protection of the people who lived in it. We were quite satisfied with the Pennsylvania man the Yankees sent as our guard. His name was Joe and reminded us of my deceased brother who was also named Joe. Guard Joe actually addressed my mother as Mother. He churned for her, peeled apples and potatoes, swept the floors, and made himself useful. He was intelligent and extremely sympathetic when he learned of the death of our own Joe.

Another group that I watched pass through town were freed slaves. They headed to Tennessee, possibly because the Yankees had come from that direction. Heading westward seemed to make more sense than heading east. There were hundreds and hundreds of free men, women, and children in an almost constant procession. Some were on horses. A rather bony horse was piled with various bundles and sacks packed with clothing. On top of the pile sat an elderly former slave, her bonnet hanging over her back, held there by its ribbons. She held the horse's reins in her hands and swayed back and forth with its movement. "Glory, glory! We's free, we's free. Glory, halleluia!"

Other people sang, too. Some laughed in the ecstasy of their freedom. All sorts of conditions, people, horses, and mules made up the procession. Some horses had saddles, others were bareback. Shouts of "Glory, glory, we's free, we's free!" filled the air even in the middle of all the confusion.

We had three servants—a house boy, a house girl, and a cook. The first two left almost immediately. However, our cook, "Aunt

George's War, Then and Now

Becky," stayed for quite a while. She even outwitted the Yankees who nosed around people's houses looking for provisions. Father had brought in a supply of flour and meat for us to use while he was away. Aunt Becky hid the supplies in a closet between the stairway and wall. Then she nailed the door shut and hung her sifter, rolling pin, and other kitchen utensils over the door. The Yankees looked around, but Aunt Becky never let on that there was anything for the soldiers to find.

Father wanted her to stay for wages, but she decided that she could not remain in her old place and be truly free. She returned to Greeneville, Tennessee, where she died of cholera in 1873.

Towards the end of the war, things looked gloomy for the Rebels. They lost hope and the soldiers were disheartened. The colonel from one regiment encamped in Asheville was rumored to no longer support the cause. As many as fifteen of his men deserted one night. They knew there were no resources to go into the mountains to look for a handful of deserters. After all, the whole army was about to collapse.

There was a large wooden building at the edge of town that the Rebels had used as an arsenal. The residents had no idea how well or poorly stocked with combustibles it was. When the Yankees decided to set the building on fire, no one knew what kind of explosion there would be. They had no idea of what damage would be caused. As it turned out, no one was injured but as the shells exploded, sounds like a small battle erupted. In a short time, the building was in ashes.

At last the war was over and the men who survived began returning home. But conditions in Asheville were bad for some time. A Yankee garrison was stationed there to protect the people and stop any potential rebellion. However, the soldiers disturbed the peace of the entire community with their drinking

A Great-Granddaughter Reflects

and keeping the saloons busy. Mad with drink, they would rush through the streets shouting blasphemies and firing their pistols. Finally, the garrison left the town which made the residents almost as happy as the end of the war.

Even though the war was over, feelings still ran high. One businessman hung the Union Stars and Stripes over the door to his establishment and across the pavement. People who had been fighting for so long against what that flag stood for were mad. They refused to walk under the flag. The store owner then decided to stretch a rope of flags from the old Eagle Hotel across the street to his store.

As one couple drove down the street, the wife exclaimed to her husband, "Don't drive under those rags!" The poor man had to drive several blocks out of the way to avoid the American flags.

The same woman owned elegant property on Battery Hill Park. She wanted to restore her gardens to their pre-war glory. She invited a renowned gardener to visit her because she was impressed with his work. She was just about to reach an agreement with him when he said something about New York. She asked, "Are you from New York?"

"I have that honor, madam," he said.

"There's the door," she said, and pointed to the exit. The gardener left, wondering if the woman knew the war was over...

The End

NOW

A Great-Granddaughter Reflects

George F. Robertson, my dad's grandfather on his mother's side, has always been a character in my life even though he died before I was born. My birth name is Elizabeth Robertson Lindsay because I was named for both of my grandmothers—Elvie **Elizabeth** Howard Barnett and Georgie Oliphant **Robertson** Lindsay.

I knew that George Robertson was a Presbyterian minister and I had even visited one of the churches he had served. My grandmother gave me many of her father's study and sermon preparatory notes. I knew that my great-grandfather had written several books. Is it just happenstance that I, with my middle name from birth as Robertson, also became a Presbyterian U.S.A. minister and a writer?

As I said in the preface, I thought for a long time that I might want to revisit the book George Robertson wrote in 1932—when he was seventy-nine years old—a book of his memories of the Civil War. Then when I finally did, I found it both insightful about the times as well as disturbing.

The Civil War was also called The War of Northern Aggression or the War Between the States, depending on which side was telling the story. Even the causes of the war were and

George's War, Then and Now

are interpreted differently. Some people believe the war was over the institution of slavery...whether it was an economic necessity, a right of property owners, or a horrible affliction on human beings. Others believe the war was over states' rights. Many southern states did not want the federal government telling them what they could and could not do.

No matter which side was speaking, slavery was a blight upon our entire country...northern and southern...although it played out in different ways. Unfortunately, as I began studying my great-grandfather's book more in depth, I realized that many of these battles are still being fought. People of color are still judged and considered "less than" by our national and local governments. Systemic racism is a reality. Battles over the display of confederate flags and monuments still bring people to question what justice is, who is being treated unjustly, and how history can align with current issues. Even though the actual war is over, the currents of bigotry, racism, and power inequities still run deep.

This book took on more life that I expected when I first began what I thought would be a simple update of my great-grandfather's little book. His words about Stars and Bars have become more poignant to me as the Confederate flag (not Stars and Bars) continues to divide people and foment hatred. People struggle with the challenges of monuments honoring people who fought to sustain slavery. I intentionally left out portions that were quite incendiary—laughter over how a slave was treated, for example. Some of the memories were laced with cultural and derogatory observations that are inappropriate today.

I must acknowledge that members of my family were slave owners, even though my great-great grandparents called

A Great-Granddaughter Reflects

their house slaves "servants." As is referenced here, offering to pay the cook-housekeeper only after slavery was abolished is understandable in the context of the time but this great-great granddaughter of George's parents is disappointed that it did not happen earlier.

Even though George's father, my great-great grandfather, was not necessarily committed to the institution of slavery, he decided to back the southern cause when many of his neighbors decided to align that way. So, he became an active part of the Confederate army. I can understand that. The pressure of those in one's community as well as financial impacts are always heavy, especially when families and children are involved.

Perhaps what fascinates me most about George's version of the Civil War is that, as a child, he did not experience war as it is often depicted. There were no battles in his tale. He shares what life was like when men in uniform and the instruments of war moved in and out of his town. The trappings of battle were fascinating to him...even when/if he did not fully comprehend the impact of the War or even the strategies of war.

George tells the stories through the eyes of a young boy, as someone who is understandably impressed with meeting a general. He plays war as so many children have done throughout the ages. He can watch how his parents like or dislike the people who moved in and out of their towns. But he tells his story as a young white boy whose version of the story would be very different from one told by an eight-year-old boy with dark skin, even though the boys might have been friends while young.

I have learned with the help of my son, David Templeton, that my great-grandfather testified in 1921 in Marvin, NC, at a trial that contested the will of two well-to-do white sisters who had left their 800 acres along with cash and a house to a black

George's War, Then and Now

man, Bob Ross, and his daughter Mittie Bell Houston. Both Ross and Houston had grown up with the sisters. Over one hundred cousins contested the will. My minister great-grandfather testified to the sanity of Miss Maggie.

Gene Stowe wrote a book about the 1921 trial as well as the second trial in 1924 titled *Inherit the Land: Jim Crow vs. Miss Maggie's Will*. The all-white jury upheld the will both times.

In our time, with the murders of George Floyd, Breonna Taylor, Ahmaud Arbery, Sandra Bland, Paul Castaway, Melissa Ventura, Eric Garner, Michael Brown, Trayvon Martin and countless others, an opportunity has been released for our country—and me—to look at systemic racism. We can decide if we truly want to live into the principles that this country was founded on: liberty and justice FOR ALL.

I grew up in the South in the 1950s when Jim Crow laws were still in effect. I asked my mom about the "White Only" sign at the water fountain in the old Sears Roebuck building. I wondered why we entered the doctor's office in one door while people with darker skin went to the door in the back. I was not raised in a totally lily-white bubble because my family interacted with people of different skin colors and nationalities.

I have devoted my life to reaching out to others: through my former work in a large nonprofit that continues to help people of various skin colors (many who live in poverty) to emerge from their hurting situations, with my writing, through teaching people with resources about poverty so they can reduce judgment and increase compassion, by working in churches, even at one time preaching twice a month for three years in an African-American congregation. When I was in seminary two men with dark skin, one American and the other Nigerian, were often

A Great-Granddaughter Reflects

guests in my home. I have worked with people of color both as staff and volunteers.

I say all of this not to say how enlightened I am but to undergird my belief that racism is deeply held at places in our spirit that are not even rational or conscious. I have wondered about this for a long time.

I went to a conference on peacemaking that focused on racism. I was astounded when the presenters, one a black woman and the other a white man, began their presentation with the white man announcing that he was a racist. (I almost left at that point.) He went on to add that he was against racism and that he was an anti-racist, but he could never call himself a non-racist. He explained that his white skin gave him privileges that he did not even know he enjoyed. They both talked about the insult of claiming to be color blind. They explained that being "color blind" means that one refuses to acknowledge a person in his/her God-given wholeness.

I used to feel enlightened regarding racism when I could proudly say I was colorblind. I enjoyed interacting with people of different color or ethnicity. I felt comfortable. I felt nonjudgmental. That is, until I learned more about diversity and systemic racism. Now I know that when I am "colorblind" to someone whose skin is darker than mine, I am discounting who they really are. I am refusing to acknowledge that their life experiences are different from mine. I am choosing to see them as just like me. What an insult to them and a loss to me!

I am still confounded, embarrassed, and horrified when I react internally to certain things. I note the increasing number of mixed-race couples on television and appreciate their presence... but I still notice. I am glad that I am aware of that in myself and can choose to move past it. I feel uncomfortable when I see a man who is different from me in skin color or socioeconomics where I was not expecting him to be. Part of this is being a woman alone but part of it is subconscious racism and classism.

I now consciously choose to be anti-racist. I yearn to discover for myself how to best respond to what is happening. I want to be a catalyst for change. I also know that putting this book out now, as important as it is for me, as well as witnessing people call for action OR participate in peaceful protests OR preach powerful sermons OR proclaim the gospel of love, only touches the surface of dealing with the centuries of exploitation, repression, and dehumanizing attitudes that are part of me in my whiteness and even my deepest self.

Fear makes us lose our best selves. Recognizing in another's face a connection that is beyond an "instinctive" response is something to strive for, pray for, and consciously work for. My current prayer is that we will not let this moment pass unnoticed AND that we will trust that true change is an ongoing intentional process for each of us and the world.

My great-grandfather's tale shows a "gentler" side of war. It also provides an opportunity for us to decide if we want to be like the woman in Asheville who continued to carry the hatred in her life or if we want to live in and work for a country with liberty and justice for all.

Acknowledgments

My father, George Denton Lindsay, was thrilled to learn before his death that I was working on this project. I received his blessing with joy.

My son, David Templeton, loves genealogy. I am grateful to him for unearthing the *Davidsonian* book review as well as information about the trial of "Jim Crow vs. Miss Maggie's will."

Thanks to grandchildren Lindsay and Michael Templeton who both read early versions of George's recollections.

My wonderful editor Vally Sharpe keeps pushing me beyond the simple little tale that I thought I was dealing with. We both allowed the manuscript to sit on a shelf until the time was right...even though neither of us knew we were waiting for this numinous time.

Thanks to all my friends, family, and readers for the nurture and support that sustains me.

About the Author
George F. Robertson, D.D.

GEORGE F. ROBERTSON was born in Greeneville, Tennessee and moved, once the Civil War started, with his family to Wytheville, Virginia, where his father had been ordered to go. The family would eventually move again, to Asheville, North Carolina, where they remained. After attending a boys school and Newton Academy, George eventually matriculated at Davidson College, started by the Presbyterian Church. He would go on to Princeton University and to King College, where he earned a Doctorate in Divinity.

In addition to becoming an author of this and other books, George would become a Presbyterian minister.

About the Author
Beth Lindsay Templeton

BETH LINDSAY TEMPLETON, Founder and CEO of Our Eyes Were Opened, Inc. is a public speaker, Presbyterian minister, retreat leader, and writer. For many years, she worked at United Ministries, a non-profit in Greenville, South Carolina, where she worked with both "the have-nots" and "the haves." Since 2007, she has focused on a ministry with "the haves" so they can enlarge their thinking about people who live in poverty in order to reduce judgment and increase compassion. Beth works with congregations, schools, universities, medical facilities, women's groups, civic groups, and businesses in Greenville and around the country. She is the author of 11 books.

Beth is a graduate of Presbyterian College and Erskine Theological Seminary. She is a mother and grandmother.

To contact Beth, email her at:

beth@oewo.org